A MONSTER

Text copyright © 2019 by Haiying Wu
Illustrations copyright © 2019 by Haibo Xu
All rights reserved, including the right of reproduction in whole or in part in any form.

Translation by Charles Nichols
English editing by Haibo Xu
Design by Haibo Xu

Chinese edition published under the title 有怪兽 by China Light Industry Press Ltd in 2022.
English translation edition published by Seaflame Children's Books with the express permission of China Light Industry Press Ltd.

The text for this book was set in Playtime With Hot Toddies, Arial and Source Han Serif.
The illustrations for this book was rendered in Chinese ink and colored digitally.

Identifies:
ISBN 978-1-7752835-3-9 (Hardcover)
ISBN 978-1-7752835-4-6 (Paperback)
ISBN 978-1-7752835-2-2 (eBook)

MONSTER

Written by
Haiying Wu

Translation by
Charles Nichols

Illustrated by
Haibo Xu

SEAFLAME
Children's Books

"What is that?"

"A monster!
A monster!"

"Quick, run away! A monster with a long tail!"

"A monster with big sharp claws!"

"Run away! A monster with tangled hair!"

Where's Little Bear?

Run Bunny!
Run Doggy!
Run Fox!
Run Elephant!

Ahhhh

呀呀

Arghhh

Ah

Argh

咕噜噜噜噜噜

Grrrrrr…

"I'm not a monster, I'm a lion. The monster is in the tree hollow and he's growling!"

It sounds like the snore of Little Bear.

嚕 嚕嚕嚕 嚕嚕嚕

GrrRrrrRrrrrrr

It is Little Bear!

He's sound asleep in the tree hollow!

鸣鸣

Little Bear is awake.

"What is going on?"

"There's no monster."

"But there's all these red footprints. Could there be…"

Haiying Wu is an award-winning author of several popular children's books. Her picture book series ***Wow! The Classic of Mountains and Seas*** was selected for the 2020 Motion Force China Original Animation Publishing Support Program, and her book ***Grandpa Likes to Hide and Seek*** won the 2017 Hsin Yi Picture Book Award. She lives in Tangshan, China and Toronto, Canada.

Charles Nichols was born in Houston, Texas in 2004 and has lived in Calgary, Alberta since 2012. He has been offered admission to the University of Toronto Faculty of Arts & Science. He has long had an interest in creative writing, aspiring to have a career as a novelist.

Haibo Xu is an illustrator and graphic designer based in Calgary, Canada. He was born in Guangdong, China and immigrated to Canada when he was 18. He graduated from the Alberta University of Arts. This is his first picture book, and it has been shortlisted for the third Little Cool Hat International Picture Book Award in 2019.

www.ingramcontent.com/pod-product-compliance
Lightning Source LLC
Chambersburg PA
CBHW041109210426

43209CB00063BA/1858